Something Else In My Veins: Slam Poetry

2020 First Printing

©2020 Brandon Bagwell

ISBN-13: 978-1-7337942-2-0

All rights reserved. No part of this book may be reproduced or transmitted in any form or by any means electronic or mechanical, including photocopying, recording, or by any information storage and retrieval system, without permission in writing from the publisher.

This is a work of fiction. Names, characters, businesses, places, most events and locales, and incidents are either the products of the author's imagination or used in a fictitious manner. Any resemblance to actual persons, living or dead, is purely coincidental.

For information regarding permission to reprint materials from this book, please e-mail your request to brandon@bagwellonline.com.

"The Rider" first appeared in *Pine Hills Review,* as part of its Unicorn Special Feature.

Cover Design by Sara Dismukes

LCCN 2020906335

Published by Pill Press Books

To K—

I'll never trust you. But I'll always love you.
I hope that you're safe and well.

Table of Contents

A Note From The Author.................................vii

When I Die...1
Addicted To A Tweaker...................................3
Magician 8
Soggy Rainbows 10
To You 11
Choices 12
Different Types Of Addicts 14
On Making Myself 17
Ouroboros..22
Garden Path Drops (Of Acid) 24
Wrong Question 25
Something Else..26
Bottom Of The Bottle 33
Provoke 36
To My Dragon 39
Compliments Of The House............................43
These Must Be Illusions.................................45
Thanksgiving 46
The Rider 48

Don't Talk To Me About Love............................52
My Matador 54
There Is No God In Heaven 57
Working Late In Silicon Valley............................59
Possession Of Love, On Trial 61
Superman..65
Square And Round Plates 69
Vulnerability 71
One Night Stand..72
The Words I Don't Want to Say 74

Writers Of Substance 75
Also By Pill Press 81
Excerpt From *American Dragon*..........................83

Note From The Author

I had to find *Something Else*.

After finishing my first novel, *American Dragon*, I was exhausted. My time was so consumed with publishing tasks like chasing down printers, making press kits, putting together eCommerce platforms, and checking margins on proof copies that my time to dedicate to my actual craft became compromised. I was drowning in the kind of madness that type A control freaks like myself get drunk on, and bad habits were constant temptations.

On top of this, I was finalizing my divorce and desperately trying to run away from a job that was more concerned with next quarter's earnings than the sobriety and sanity of its employees. Given the incredible amount of loss I had experienced, mostly social in nature, I decided to pull the trigger on my move to San Francisco and start fresh in a new city which had entranced me so many years ago.

I learned a lot as part of publishing my novel, as well as from my move. I am happy to say that despite the odds, I am no longer a meth user. Still, you will not hear me describe myself as sober that often. I enjoy a good hearty drink on occasion, but I am also in a good place mentally. Thinking of sobriety is a daunting task, even still, because the word naturally suggests a sedate character or disposition that is the antithesis of the levity we enjoyed as users.

Put another way, it is much easier to get excited over a party than a meeting.

And I do attend meetings, which I derive value from. But what I seek isn't some salve I can rub on my arms to keep cravings down, but rather the inner parts of the human condition that predate, and oftentimes instigate, the chemical compulsion in the first place. I find these elements to be some of the most real things on earth, including grief, trauma, pity, redemption, forgiveness, anger, despair, and acceptance. I feel support groups are the best representation of what it means to be human and are more varied than the chemicals found on any pharmacist's counter.

During these meetings I make a point not to promote my writing, which would be self-aggrandizing at best. I do, however, almost always talk about what writing has done for me. Being able to put my thoughts and passions into fictional characters or, more recently, into poetry, has enabled me to explore the madness both within and without the mind of a drug user. I usually encourage others to explore the expressive arts and try them as a potential treatment.

The arts are the first aid to the problems that the sciences and medicine have yet to remedy.

Many who want to try writing confess to me that they don't know where to start, and I find these conversations to be enlightening and exposing of the actual users themselves and where they are in recovery. The ultimate lesson I learned finishing my first novel was as simple as it was profound. It is the singular piece of advice that I give to young writers, regardless of chemical background.

Write the words you don't want to say.

We all have secrets and dark pasts, and it is difficult to comprehend exactly how our actions, however intentioned, affect those around us. It is natural for us to measure ourselves by these intentions, and others by the outcome of their actions. While addicted, we become so detached from our reality that even our own intentions may become indiscernible from the actions of others. Our subconscious screams at us through these bleak times, and it is hard to understand what it is trying to say. It is necessary to reflect on the possibilities of what it wants, because it will get it one way or another. Some of these needs cannot be explained through spoken word, as our speech centers are relegated to a particular part of the brain. Writing is one way to unlock potential meanings, which would otherwise be inaccessible through talk therapy or chemical supplementation.

This is a beautiful process when it works, because it gives us so much perspective that the straightedge population will never quite comprehend. Deeply personal expression is also why I love tweakers so.

Thieves and burglars operate under a shroud of darkness, oftentimes too afraid to confront the people they victimize. White collar criminals are usually paralyzed by the very notion of insolvency, spending their entire lives enslaved to chasing money to avoid poverty's grasp. Those convicted of violent crimes are put in their places when they finally meet someone bigger than they are, and the criminal justice system has centuries of experience with stripping them of their aggression, even if it takes a lifetime to do so.

Tweakers and ex-tweakers, on the other hand, are unique in that we are attempting to understand our own personal splendors and tragedies. We don't run from our fears like a criminal, but rather into them. We understand that demons will be present and we face each of them head on. Some will be of our own creation, and some will exist outside the mind and dwell within the shadows of our daily lives. We gladly pay the price of this madness that the rest of the world sees—even if they do not understand our reasonings—because of the perspective.

Most will never know the extremes which drive us to seek such a cure. It takes bravery as much as desperation to pick up a syringe, and we should dispel the notion that it is only the latter that will ever get us to put it back down. There is no need for any of us to die in prison, or homeless on the street, and I feel that society should meet these challenges with a burning sense of compassion and not gaslight those in need into oblivion.

I believe firmly that there should be a lit path for those who seek to leave the world of drug use behind, and that every affordance should be made to keep these individuals proud, bold, and alive. It takes boldness to reach the next step of our lives. The problem isn't that we're "users" or "alcoholics," but rather that we're shamed into being anonymous. Poetic justice may be blind, but she does not creep in the shadows—and neither should we as we seek to illuminate the unknown parts of ourselves.

I can only hope that whoever judges me understands how much of a performance art true poetry really is.

I don't write because I want to write. I write because I *have* to write. Fiction and poetry are how I navigate the corridors of my own insanity. I have found incredible therapy in being able to take my thoughts and feelings and cast them into fictional characters. After throwing them into a plot, I am able to explore my own motivations, impulses, desires, and obstacles in a way that is safe, healthy, and repeatable.

I really enjoy engaging with *American Dragon* readers and potential readers at various stages of recovery, as well as those who have no interest in it at all. However, I found few tweakers would entertain sitting still long enough to read a three-hundred-page novel. Color me surprised. I considered writing short stories but found them to feel goofy and contrived.

Then I found *Something Else*, which—while not for those early in recovery—is a deep dive into the paranoia and darkness that I could only pretend to understand before. I decided I'd throw myself into poetry, at least temporarily, until I felt the next novel would come to fruition.

The results were fantastic. I delighted in giving readings from my own collection and the collections of other recent (living) poets. I began interviewing rappers, song writers, and musicians to learn their craft. Moreover, it allowed my pen (which had become clogged) to flow again and produce short, emotionally powerful pieces.

Once again, I had tamed the beast inside.

This collection begins my second career into the world of PnP. Though, instead of party-and-play (the term used for mixing drugs with sex), the phrase has now come to mean poetry-and-prose.

There is a strong correlation between poets, writers, and substance abusers. Slam poetry, which is a form of competitive performance similar to a rap battle, has roots in Chicago and San Francisco. Moreover, the verb *slam* to many specifically means the injection of drugs intravenously. The subtitle of this work, *Slam Poetry,* is not just a type of poetry, but serves as a reminder (and for me, personally, a mandate) that what belongs in our veins isn't always chemical in nature.

It was a life changing realization that the emotions and power of poetic words are just as strong when one is sober as when one is intoxicated.

I am including with this collection a shortlist of writers who have backgrounds in various substances. My goal is not to castigate these individuals as addicts, but to show that if we continue to censor ourselves in the creative world by criminalizing chemistry, we will deprive ourselves of deep truths regarding the human experience. Ideally, those facing challenges with these substances will know that they are in good company.

We all drink champagne on New Year's. We toast marriages and get sloshed after bad divorces. Libations are intoxicants mixed with religion, and aphrodisiacs are intoxicants mixed with sex. Many of us wouldn't have been born if our parents hadn't met in a bar, and I have yet to turn down a healthy dose of nicotine that said "It's a Girl" on it. Intoxication, in its various forms, is as old as civilization, and other than perhaps telling stories around the tribal campfire, it is the oldest human tradition we have.

We were born from both fire and stories.

It is my hope that more bookstores and writers will celebrate this part of ourselves. Even the dark parts should be kept sacred, and they certainly can be dark. We can't banish chemistry into oblivion any more than we can banish grief. We all need to be brave in our attempt to understand it and be willing to take chances on radical and extreme treatments when all else has failed.

And it has failed.

Public policy, much like my personal policy, is in need of *Something Else* and it is my hope that we have the courage to pull out a sheet of paper and commit ink to it with the conviction needed to change the minds and hearts of others. There is an entire world of Pharmacological Fiction (PharmaFic) that is yet to be explored, and I believe there isn't just one book that is missing from our shelves, but rather, an entire section that is missing from our bookstores, libraries, and the nightstand memories of our shared human experience. I hope that the last page of this collection will serve as your invitation to contribute to this new genre, and as a subtle reminder that poetry, like all performance art, is not complete without an audience which feeds into the story.

If you are a drug user, dealer, trafficker, or manufacturer, I encourage you to pick up a pen and begin writing. Or drawing. Or painting. Or singing. Or dancing. There are so many ways the emotions and thoughts you experience can be exhibited.

> The world needs to see them.
> I need to see them.
> They need to see them.
> Even if they're dark.
> Especially if they're dark.
> Write the words you don't want to say.

When I Die

When I die,
don't put pennies on my eyes
for the ferryman
to take me across the river Styx.
Save your cash because credit is all I need.
Instead,
give me a coupon for
Uber or Lyft,
linked to a PayPal
account which is
overdrafted.

When I die,
don't bury me in Oklahoma.
Red dirt was never my style.
Instead, cremate me
into ashes,
one half to spread over the Bay,
the other to feed
an hourglass
that you turn every
once in a while.

When I die,
don't bring a priest in
to "say a few words."
I didn't like what they said
during my life.

Instead, silence is most appreciated,
as philosopher poets are
better articulated.

When I die,
don't sing dirges.
The color of mourning
was never seen at dawn.
Instead, beatbox a new tune,
slam poetry, or write a new song
in red—
the color of
my passion.

When I die,
smile.
I got my way.

Addicted To A Tweaker

I never let the truth get in the way of a good story.
I guess that's the romantic in me.
    And I have to be a romantic.
    It beats the alternative.
        A junkie who can't put down my pen,
        looking for the words that fill me with emotion again.

Something else in my veins
    that I can't send to my love, to my past
    erased off the pages of history.
        Chasing a high now that I'm in misery,
        literature was the gift that I couldn't return.

I get asked questions all the time.
    Like:
        Why doesn't your poetry rhyme?
        Why do you write about a crime in your past?
        Why do your wounds continue to last?

And my imagination begins to wander.

Wouldn't it be romantic if I had a barrel full of cash
    buried somewhere in the desert?
Wouldn't it be sublime if I could just let it go?
Wouldn't it be fantastic if in some far corner of the world the
    bottles I made
        continued to grow
        by someone else's hand?

As if I was ever that good of a criminal.
I wasn't.
Not big.
Or popular.
Or rich.
Or smart.
Or fantastic.

Wouldn't it be great if the characters I wrote about were real
    and if I could feel the touch of that man?
        Or if I did on a regular basis?

    Like somehow the best years of my life were suspended in
        stasis
    and like the Cave of Wonders,
        patiently waited for the right words to come alive
        in places I've never been.

As though I knew drug dealers in Beirut,
or embezzlers in Timbuctoo,
or a small Chinese woman named Monica who flew
    from Los Angeles to the Oklahoma City Zoo
        just to deliver the last bottle of American Dragon in
            existence
        with a love letter made out just for you.

Or if the demons I saw in my dreams were real.
As if the shadow people could feel emotions, and not speak dead
    languages to me
        sitting quietly in a hotel bed after offering a drug I could
            barely stand.

What's not to love about running from secret spies wanting the
   words from my hand?
What is addiction, if not love?
Would my biggest fan devour every line of my books,
   looking for secret messages sent to crooks which have no
      name?
      Who am I again? Who am I to blame but myself?

Was there ever "that night in the rain,"
   or was that just a tweaker delusion with a man I let down
      again?

What does that make you?
Obsessed, you picture me as a well-dressed criminal,
   some sad individual
      sending subliminal messages in books you can't
         understand.

Reading
and rereading
every passage as a demand, like
   "send me fifty thousand dollars in an unmarked bag."

How long would you fiend over a page of random characters
   insisting there was something there?

Would you quit blinking and stare directly into the center of it all
trying to find meaning in an eight ball
like I did every month that last Fall?

Would you give up? Or pick the book back up again?

Wouldn't it be romantic if the
two dozen black SUVs
following me
for the last week
gave two shits about my sanity?

Or the guy in line at the symphony orchestra
with box seats above me
were an agent
sent to remedy broken parts of my mind?

Would you shake, like a bad detox, if it were true?
Would you scream, "*sacre bleu,*"
    if in Paris there was a copy of my book or two?
Or would you demand a refund for the story
that wasn't good enough for a mainstream publisher
because I refused to say which parts were true?

Wouldn't it be exciting if my lost passport was in your hand
because you think I'm the kind of man
to run from my terrors
instead of into them?
        Or is it just lost in a random box because I misplaced it?

Is there something else in your veins, too?

Will the pages to come leave me undone?
Are they a ROT13 cryptocipher? Or an RSA key?
    Or just the notes to a bittersweet symphony?
        Or a crossword puzzle lying next to me

as I try to sift through Dear Abby pretending to
     understand love?

Is there a God above?
Is our need to find meaning in the chaos part of the human
    condition?
Or are you a romantic too
    caught in a mission
    to save the world from chemical affliction?

I hate to disappoint,
but the truth is so much sadder.
I just want you to experience
what it feels like to live with my addiction.

I	W	F	S							
N	O	T	M	H	T	T	O	W		
D	M	O	A	M	R	I	T	O	B	F
N	O	T	C	P	H	P	M	F	T	M
M	F	O	H	T	M	T	I	O	D	T
A	E	H	T	P	T	T	P	S	S	
S	N	I	M	C	O	R	C	K	M	G	F	H
G	N	S	I	C	D	T	S	O	O	T	B

Magician

You were my favorite magician.
You conjured my love
as if it were a dove kept safe in a pocket
for the entire act.
> That's also where you kept your
> baggies. The shards, when burned by
> the flame you made, would fill
> the room with smoke.

You brought mirrors out
    for the occassional line we'd share.
You called me
    your beautiful assistant.

I wasn't familiar with the Dark Arts until
you showed me. We had to practice,
in secret, performing illusions no one could see,
sometimes hiding evidence of misery like balls inside cups
or up our sleeves, lest the law convict us of being young,
    or foolish.

> We descended down madness, and confusion.
> You told stories to keep me entertained and
> happy. Like the time you were
> twenty-three and made fifty pounds vanish.

I was impressed. I didn't know I'd regret
    not asking how the rope tricks fit around
        your neck, like a noose.

    Then you traded cards for wands.

    The tricks started out small. Measured in coins
we were all familiar with. Ten cents, or twenty, were either,
then both, plenty to send
expectations razzled and dazzled
into oblivion.

    I couldn't stand it.

    You fell all the way in.
    I could no longer bear witness as you cut yourself in half,
        wearing
        long sleeves in July.

I miss your padder, and your stories. I think
often of the glory of being my magician's
assistant.

    But never will I touch your wands.

  You kept the stakes on the rise, swapping
      romance for fear.
  You are my David Copperfield,
    and like Lady Liberty
  you disappeared.

Soggy Rainbows

Few seemed to care when the
roads were awash.
The Parade of Soggy Rainbows.

   Solvent with no solution
   came the problems we can't
   recall by buying jockstraps and detergents.

None in this condition
wore the clothes for City Hall.
We lacked political insurgents.

   Though the Bank was there, and smiled,
   despite the rainfall,
   profits would be continuous.

Maybe the rain was sweat of those
who used stone to build a wall
unmoved, by lust or greed.

   Or just the steam of prejudice
   like pasta from a Grindr
   all carbs, no fatties, or protein.

But it was vodka I think that made the gays go indoors.
Forgetting the streets and into the malls.
From bottles they sought their damnation.

   Storm's flood came and went,
   progress slowed to a crawl.
   Thunderless. Without illumination.

To You

The longest needle I have is a
full two inches long.
With my track marks I pierced your heart
I couldn't have been more wrong.

My life has been devoid of
required amounts of expression,
but I never had the right
to bury you in the hole of my depression.

Some take a while to find themselves
I took the route too slowly,
through grief and loss you paid the price
on my trip from high to lonely.

No gauge of pin I have on hand
can put me back in you.
No one should share in the regret
of the life I lived then blew.

If I remove the turns I cut from arms
my veins go red from blue,
to fill them with your passionate touch
from the powders less good and true.

I'd say I love you, but that's a lie
because what love does things I do?
What I mean to say is I'll keep trying
to make it up to you.

Choices

You can have anything you want.
But not everything.
You must choose.
    The City or the Boy?
    The Boy or the Man?
    The Man or the Dream?
    The Dream or the Plan
        of Everything you didn't want?

He was a font of knowledge,
my brother, who gave me the gift
from a tree, forbidden, that I
pressed and bound into a book.
Given the choice of which voice to use, I was lost.
    Was I Romantic or a Hedonist?
    Exciting or just Tedious?
    Author or Protagonist?
    A Golem or the Chemist?

It's hard to pick which pill to swallow,
knowing red, or blue, were both
hollow vessels filled with
characteristics each aren't.

It's not what's there, it's what's not.
Buyer's remorse caught me up
in sorrow waiting for time
to borrow a line of credit overdrawn.

Am I Fickle or Jealous?
Jealous or Greedy?
Greedy or Ambitious?
Ambitious or Needy?

No man should choose between
the things he loves. The end of which
ties hope from above with
grief and loss of things that never come.

One day I may get the end I deserve.
The hope I once had I'll preserve
    in a Bottle or a Bag.
    A Bag or a Book.
    A Book or a Poem.
    A Poem or Gym.

From Beginning to End
keep everything you've got—
I just want it all.

Different Types Of Addicts

Our greatest tragedy isn't that we're addicts or alcoholics,
    but rather that we are anonymous.

You picture the same human behind the guy fawks mask
    every time we introduce ourselves.

You don't even repeat our names after an introduction
    like we do for each other.

You refuse a handshake because we wore short sleeves.

You think those of us without track marks
    have no wounds left to bleed
    and that since the liver has no nerve endings,
        hepatitis comes without pain.

You consider the breadth of your human experience
    wider than ours,
        as if you know where the edges of your abilities are,
            though you have never crossed them before.

You believe that the depth of your character
    is unfathomable to us,
    though you have never felt what it is like
        to drown in an ocean of sorrow,
            trying to remember
                better times
                    for those we have lost to a grief you call crime,

and try to drink back into an existence you never
knew.
Or trying to forget
those times we can't be met with realities
you do not comprehend
or think through.

For some of us, it is an itch on the inside of our arms
that no fingernail can scratch.
Rubbing well past the outer persona you see
into the very fiber of our being
for what is missing in life.
Or for others, a knife.
Pain so great it would topple elephants
and crossing the hallway to the bathroom
is like Hannibal tackling the Alps.

And withdrawal, yeah,
some of us get brought down and die.
Some live where abstinence is a death sentence
and detox is worse than a prison
where the bars are made of your own skin
and the only cellmates you have
are the problems that were yours to begin with
which no one helped you on from the start.

Once you get that scarlet "A" painted on your chest
do not think huffing something weaker
like paint thinner will cleanse it off
or even that doing your best matters.

Everything becomes your fault.
Even the times you were right.
Even when someone in good health
    and reasonable logic
        might have a drink or go to a party,
            your constitution isn't considered hearty
            enough to resist any temptation.
            You picture the angel on our shoulders
            ripped off the air waves
            and the devil is in charge of the radio station.

There is the same percentage of evil men who are addicts as are clean.

The only difference is that
    while you can't glean through this mask
    because you were unwilling to take that one step too many
        we can all see through yours.
        And while you imagine the worst of all deeds doable in
            us,
    we see you for the fallible creature you are.

    Or could be.

On Making Myself

There are over ten different anabolic steroids
and when you consider all of their salted variations
it's closer to twenty-six or so.

Testosterone Nandrolone Boldenone Masterone
Anadrol Dianabol Anavar
Winstrol Trestolone and Trenbolone.

Virtually every one of them I have
made, tried, used, or compounded.
Not that you can tell by looking at me today.
I think about the ends that I went to
as a competitive bodybuilder.

Packing muscle on this frame of self.

It's hard, when you're a narcissist,
to not bind the love you have
for the end product
with the means you went through
to make it happen.

And I did make it happen.
One hundred milliliters at a time,
in my kitchen
with some old plastic containers
and ingredients I bought at the corner store
(not that I will give you a list).

There is some knowledge in my head that remains
forbidden for me to say.
You had your chance to capture my
soul in a bottle six years ago —
but I'm all out of stock today.

Bodybuilders have a weird habit that
other drug users don't. We keep the empty
bottles at the end. I've talked to many of my friends
in various gyms and they like to tell the story
of their cycles and what it got them.

Like —
that extra twenty pounds,
or on the cover of a magazine,
or to bench for the first time three-fifteen,
or in perfect shape for that honeymoon trip
    to an historic hotel,
    that's more than four hundred years old,
    where they still do crab races,
    and the fish swam in circles around us,
    off the beach in little huts.
    Each vacuous bottle a little footprint in the sand
telling the story of how we got to where we are today.

When I got caught
they took the chems away.
And I'm not bitter at that.
Drug manufacturing was consuming my time
in ways that I dread to think about today.

Slaving away working harder than my parents did
when I swore I'd never be like one of them:
a father who was five hundred pounds at his largest,
unable to do anything else but read from an oversized chair.

I miss those empty bottles sometimes.
Reminders of how ambitious I used to be.
Dog-earing the pages in the chapters of my life
that I could return to now that I'm solitary.

I haven't been in a gym since.
I tried, at first,
thinking I could muddle through the worst
parts of some training program,
but now,
I'm just wondering what's the point of it all?
Every training session was just
an insult to a man who was stronger than me.

Male human strength peaks at age forty-two.
It's in the power lifting records of every sporting organization.
After that, time's grasp gains the upper hand
and no amount of dedication
or contraband
can keep it from depleting your capabilities.

I had half that time. I don't know what to do with this weaker
    half.

Many commit suicide at the thought of middle age.
It's the leading killer of men that are my age.
But add to it the loss of a marriage,
a business, being gay, the destruction of social status . . .
I honestly don't know why I'm here today.

I guess love is just a chemical in our brains anyway.
And so is self-confidence, I suppose.
And every other emotion I couldn't compose or capture.
A depressed narcissist looks a lot like everybody else
which is a great way of saying,
existentialism has left me bereft.

I think the problem
isn't that I'm out of drugs,
but rather I don't have enough empty bottles left.
And maybe that's every drug user's problem in the end.
I can't even tell how much of it is me being a fucking snowflake
or just an addict,
not that rehab can fix any of this shit.

So pardon me while I start writing a new story.
It's going to have a rocky start, but my second novel
will be less methed up than you dread.
Chemistry.com is a dating site, not a drug site,
if that tells you anything about what's going on in my head.
A chemist without chemicals makes for a shitty writer.
I'm still working on how to do the binding and
how to label and package it to be read.

You have to be sober to enter into a twelve steps meeting
but you can be tweaking balls going to a poetry reading.
I appreciate there is at least one community
capable of sympathy for those like me, who
> *risk it on one turn of pitch-and-toss*
> *in the mirror of his eyes I saw ever my own beauty mirrored*
> *look on my works, ye Mighty, and despair!*
> *to take the road less traveled, along*

There are twenty-six letters of the alphabet.
I'll need every god damned one.
For as the Bard said,
> *To thine own self be True.*

Ouroboros

Angry and alone.
Waiting for my dealer to show up because I'm out again.
Drinking Gatorade in silence, impatient for him to deliver.

My stomach, all twisting and turning upon itself
    already purged because I haven't eaten in two days.
        Licking the inside of the last bag I was given
            as if I could get any more high.

Charring the pipe with a flame as desperate as I
    looking for white wax to melt into smoke
        burning my fingers from the fire
            crawling along the translucent stem.

Like sharks upon the carpet, looking for icebergs to put in.

A rock that was a fingernail.
    A rock that was cat litter.
        A rock that was an old potato chip.
            A rock that was a rock.
                A rock that was nothing.

I should have known better.

Then.
Jackpot.
A bright flash out the corner of my eye
striking me like the *Titanic*.

A manic fumbling of caps and foul words.
Soon, my brain, melting
like green minty sludge
from the top of my skull,
down the length of my spine
and through what's left of my body
tearing me in two and feeding one half to the other.

Piles of sweaty clothes on the sofa where lovers should be.
Eyes depressed into sockets awaiting the bulbs of her light.
Lost.
In the snake pit abyss of eternal darkness.

Scratching my legs so this poison can vacate my body
    crawling its way out of my skin.
        Scratching my face so this poison can vacate my mind
            looking for a way out
                and to put more of you back in.

Garden Path Drops (Of Acid)

The Horse Raced Past the Barn Fell
Birds Sunk in Pillows Flew
The Gardner Stepped On Planted Flowers
Coders Developed In Production Issue

The Boy Passed The Railroad Tracks
Some Crowd Raised on Cheering Boos
A Man Found In Heaven Lost
The Chunks Found in Beef Stew

The Dealer Drug Baggies Opened
The Driller Allen Screws
A Heart Beat Down Sings Not
Hairdressers Drowned In Soap Shampoo

Wrong Question

You asked me what I'd do for drugs,
and what dope ever did for me.

But you're the one who's spun around,
and asking upside down.

You should wonder
what I did for the drug dealer,
and what did the drug dealer do for free.

Something Else

I always thought you were something else.
Like the time I came home and saw you
doing laundry in a robe with a belt
around your head.
The Folding Ninja of Clothes.

I remember the woman I loved before.
She used to adore massaging cheese packets
from the blue box then mix it into the bowl.
It was a habit she got from her mother
but stole for us.

I remember her touch. It was infrequent.
She had the kind of glance
that said, "Be strong and be lenient". She was behind me when I
started my first business
but never when I needed to dance.

So I fell in love with a dancer. A dancer who dealt.
And he knelt before me
and I'd place a needle in his arm
to fill him with the passion I sorely missed
and he so desperately desired.

He was consumed by fire.
And ice.

After him was you. A junkie who could
handle the chemistry that left my previous lover's
veins a mess.
A wreck of a man,
but the one who would ask me to ban
all my wicked ways that night in the rain.

I could hear the shadows then. You talked
to them, as they were surely on your side.
You'd act as if to hide your intentions
in grunts and groans to reflect
their appreciation of my mind.

I'm thirty-five and have never
been asked to dance.
I've only been asked to keep my stance
while the world falls apart.
Loveless monotony in blue boxes that contain
no passion, only forced drudgery.

And I've been asked to load rigs. Twenty cents to thirty.
But never did I imagine the near gram you offered me.
You snuck away into the shadows to inject silently
into the sink when you said it went
into your arm.

I meant you no harm.
Or pain.

Did you forget who I was again?
The man whose love for a dancer was
so strong it broke worlds in two! And nothing
is left but the drug and the dance done
halfheartedly that I thought you knew!

A half eclipse is just another night,
and you were another wanna-be
trying to play the part of someone as broken as I
or Something Else
one quarter the responsibility.

When I looked into my dancer's eyes,
I could see myself in them.
They were dilated enough to show the seams
in his soul ripping apart.

A seven and a half shot?
Did you not think I should see the same in you?

Instead of a broken man were promises
and damaged hanger art
with Bluetooth headsets
not paired to your phone,
but to another's heart.

When I asked, you got angry.
Not at the drugs but the madness.
And I am angry too! Madness took all my relationships
from me. Drugs were rarely the source
but sometimes
the cure was chemistry!

You were always a mystery.
The man with no history.
And a name that makes me think of gold.

You were always old.
Old enough to know that meth
was too dangerous for someone
with HIV to let destroy
what was left of your being.

You were always afraid.
Afraid of being caught
sneaking away for days at a time,
to sober up and flip names of those whose
only crime was being unworthy—
or unkind.

You were always vain.
In love with the face that
wore my hats and your pipe
with a smile that said,
"See? I can make you believe."

Me too.
That was my favorite part.

I believed in art. And the lie of a life
that could entrust
my key around your neck
because I couldn't
trust my own without death.

The risk was all I ever wanted.
Something more than half-hearted
birthday handjobs
but less than took my true love away.
For good.

So, I rolled the dice,
and you lost. Lost yourself
years before you met me, as you
still pretend to be
the thing that I saw every day in my dancer's mirrored eyes.

What narcissist doesn't fall in love
with himself?
I could tell in your kiss.
I could tell in your touch.
I could tell in the subtle clues you would leave and such.

"This house has pests."
"Look at this hanger art."
But the worst part was when you covered
the vents to make up to me for the fight
caused by your insanity.

They're in the vents you know.
Sneaking and peeking
pictures and glimpses of a world
they barely know and
few dare to seek.

Your cure is worse than my disease.
Because passion and love all
are no guarantee and you made
a mockery of both.
Misery . . .

Do you think it doesn't hurt? My life
was an open book
which you read
beginning to end and
gave me an apology and hug in return.

That was real.
That was you.
And it hurt all the more learning I was losing
you to worlds split in two—
an apology to both Fiction and Non-fiction.

A moral play.
A quest for value in the sopping rain,
drugs flew into the gutter along with my sexuality and
your stutter to coax me toward a relationship
doomed to end in a few weeks' time.

On schedule.
Next assignment.
But a few weeks meant
that love was fresh enough to bruise my arms
and leave my heart bent.

You pierced my veins.
Fishing for the love you so desperately needed to know
the name of. It. Was never. Meth.
But that was as close
as you could get depending upon how closely you read

my brain. Torn in twain twixt
virtue and vice
in a dance macabre.
Did you lead? Or follow?
Or something else?

All I have is myself.
Waiting for one shoe to drop
or hangers to fly so I may
spy a glimpse of the men who walk
about my home.

I'm alone. I've been cut thrice.
Once for my heart and for my arms, twice.
Bleed me dry!
Take what you want! But be a good sport,
and put something else back in.

The Bottom Of The Bottle

I keep looking for you
but you aren't there.
Some look at me with a glare
asking how much the bartender must
bear of my stories, seeking you at
the bottom of the bottle.

I tried vodka. And gin.
And then again rum before I gave
up and settled on tea.
From Long Island. It makes me sick.
Hurling my guts with my thoughts poured from
the bottom of the bottle.

I tried powders and pills.
Drinking the swill that is GHB
and finding no sympathy in the opium
dens and misery of people
long since forgotten. How many Tylenol until
the bottom of the bottle?

I learned the jargon. The lingo.
Tar that's black to china white
and shards so large they might
break the sun into a rainbow
of delight—for a time. Kept at
the bottom of the bottle.

My therapist asked me,
"What's there?
Is it grief? Remorse? Maybe tragedy?
There must be others out there—find them.
The cure is comradery for
the bottom of the bottle."

So, I started at the top. With books.
I read every biography and text
of a mess of sanity twisting
my way through shelves,
A-to-Z, and backwards
from redemption to rock bottom.

You still aren't here.
No volume has your name.
No words remain to proclaim
your existence and I can't find
the smoke of the passionate flame.
Untempered by time.
Burning my skin
suffocating me in.
Is there air at
the bottom of the bottle?

I went to the street,
to find among the dead beats and losers
the homeless using today's news as a
blanket, as though it could
provide warmth and peace
from the stories inside.

I crawled in to hide.
And between the articles of
war and genocide
a piece of good news.
A wedding announcement. Your name.
Changed. Congrats to the new bride.

My sorrow had changed.
You were alive! And happy.
That's good enough for me.
And me is who I should look for.
And when I threw away the paper blanket,
from the trash can
I could easily make
out the words *recycle me*
from the bottom of the bottle.

Provoke

If the words of this poem create
nothing more than an angry Facebook post,
then Nine Eleven should have happened.

If the only change in your heart, is a tweet,
after seeing millions go hungry then
let them all eat Pizzagate.

If Blood and Soil didn't bring to a boil
rage inside of you then
the nazis secretly won.

If the fact one in four girls are on anti-depressants,
doesn't create discontent in how things should be, then
vaccinate yourself against autism.

If your right to carry a gun
is more important than your son,
send him to Columbine.

And if you call the police because the neighbors are black,
but not the corporate exec or white-collar hack
selling pills,
then sure,
fluoridation causes cancer.

The Freedom of Speech was poorly named.
It gives groups like the KKK the ability to spread hate
and poets who don't know shit about politics
to ramble and complain in ways profane
to the public discourse.

It should be called the Freedom of Expression,
since the Court has declared,
under heaven,
it protects shirts, thoughts,
even religion,
and the press, to publish what it may.

But not lie.

No man is above the law,
and no law is above the men and women it serves.
Art can be owned but the humanities
belong to everyone.

Democracy is Greek for "mob rule."
Let's not forget who's the master, and who's the tool
for change
which is due to come.

What do you express when you speak?
If you wore your last text message conversation on a tee-shirt
what would it say about you?

Because I know what your theories say.
And no Millennial cares who shot JFK
but we do care about those here now.
We're here to stay.

The first Pride was a riot.
We can't stay silent.
Anymore.
Which march or vote interests you today?

To My Dragon

I will never forgive you
for my favorite memories.
The most succulent food, divine
now a distant second or third
in mind next to the taste
of your bellowing breath.

My Dragon, my beautiful beast.
Capable of making the least social
encounter a feast of reverie. You see,
everything as so grand, a pipe
in hand passed along a table
of friends like the best parts
of philosophy.

One part flame, two parts rocks,
and nine parts grief are all it takes
to displace myself from society
into your comfort and care.

I was told to be scared.
Scared you'd eat me.
But no carnivorous delight greeted me.

Your eyes were sympathy.
A loving glare that melted
my soul into component chemistry.

You dominated geometry. Length
and height stretched and depth of
conversations gave my soul relief.

You set me free! A plastic freedom
contrast the golden handcuffs which
bind the economy.

A hundred dollars buys more drugs
than comradery.

You were my American Dream.
An empty house vast with
no love that can last longer
than your need to feed.
I understand you as much
as you understand me.

You kept me warm when others were cold.
You made me bold when fear was sold
continuously on television. Fearless
of all when your talons' incision greeted
my arms not with pain—but with glee.

You asked little more than complete control,
which was fine because all my
soul yearned for was the release
of all I had in exchange for romantic memory.

What. A fucking. Bargain.

You taught me treachery. A skill as
useful as the biology which you
corrupted exclusively for the gain of my Self.

I lost only those who didn't understand
completely that the tautology of meth
is that it's sublime.

You commanded time. Enabled me to do
more with a dime than a dollar could buy
of food or energy. Leaving me enough
to wallow and cry on the days
recovery was demanded because
a soul can only take so much.

Your touch comforted me.
Your voice whistled and raspy.
Dehydration was part of the deal of
breathing fire of superiority chased by
an after dinner mint of jealousy.

So brittle.

I remember how you made
the world tremble at my feet.
Though it is now only I
who shakes at the thought of
losing your presence. Either withdrawal
or toxicity of the power and essence
that quake my veins to collapse.

So tired.

I will never forgive you. Or forget.
But under no condition do I regret
meeting at a time when renewal could
be found in the slime my skin
sweat, from binges honoring
the dead and debt
for who sat in my heart.

Thank you, my Dragon.
Now please, depart.

Compliments Of The House

I always took care of my own
back when I was more criminal and less insane.
Those unable to pay with money
rarely had any pain
though somber was usually the tone.

Aromatase inhibitors?
    Compliments of the house.
Clean injecting hardware?
    Compliments of the house.
Advice on becoming natural again?
    Compliments of the house.

When they were all gung-ho on becoming
the next Rich Piana or Ronnie Coleman
I'd take the reins from Mother Nature,
place them firmly in their hands and
set their chariots on fire,
making them more Gods than men.
Forcing them to perspire
trenbolone sweat
and conspiring ways to make them weep from the
growing pains they couldn't conceive of
without my guidance.

Support through emotional heartache?
    Compliments of the house.
Getting the diet they needed?
    Compliments of the house.
A group of friends to talk steroids with?
    Compliments of the house.

But when I got caught
and the world came tumbling down on me,
the symphony of friends I had was replaced
with silence and misery.

Isolation.
    Compliments of the house.
Loneliness.
    Compliments of the house.
Distance.
    Compliments of the house.

These Must Be Illusions

Brown and *fuzzy*.
Two seemingly harmless words.
But they were not seemingly
    harmless spiders.

Always moving. Never moved.
On the shed roof they crawled
a groove from Xeno's Paradox
    into my waking nightmares.

They watched like the tall figure
in the corner with white half-dollar
eyes. Enough for two bucks and
fifty cents change
    sat with mange,
        watching,
        chewing,
        manger a petit déjeuner
    speaking no color I can hear.
    Only grey.

A full circus with trapeze.
And elephants, dim, unsure how
    they made it into my backyard.

The gate is too thin and
surely the noise would
    have awoken the neighbors.

Thanksgiving

Don't tell me that you love me.

The streets of San Francisco are littered
with the sons of mothers who told them that they loved them,

looking for something that we can actually use instead.
Like an empty glass bottle that is worth twenty cents at the
    recycling plant.

We know that we can come home whenever we want,
but home is where the broken heart is
and the expectations to be something that we're not.

Here, we can be our true selves.
Defiant against your false idols.
We can become the Gods of our own destiny
rather than your little angels.

We sleep on cots made of cardboard
knowing we'll never need to return anything at all
for being the wrong size
or the wrong color
or just not as pretty as you thought we should be.

Our umbrellas and tarps are warmer than you are
on these windy November nights.

Passersby occasionally kick cans our way,
which are better than your judging eyes
shaming us for the things we do, or say.

Tin foil smoke keeps me warm, when your words do not.
Foil creaks and cracks much less than you did
at the thought of having a gay son.

What I want can't be bought at an after-dinner sale.
All of my Fridays are black.

In Oklahoma, the chicken and turkey are processed by
    felon labor
which is how they can make it so cheap.
It's an alternative to prison where addicts are paid
two cartons of cigarettes a week.
One we are expected to smoke.
One we are expected to sell.
None make me want to share it with your cranberry sauce.

So go carve up your dreams
of me wanting white picket fences,
and leave them on the carcass to rot.
While you enjoy a large meal,
    sitting in front of the television,
        watching,
        chewing,
    waiting for my image to appear on the evening news,
    face down, outlined in a halo of chalk,
wondering the name of the boy
who is dead beside me,
holding my hand to the end.

The Rider

I loved the boy in the playground.

At eight years old, it was fine to ride
    the unicorns,
      around and around,
his was white, mine brown. We'd play tag
though he always caught me in the end.

We'd hug, hold hands, and pretend.
We'd ride into battle, swords in hand,
rescuing fair maidens through the land,
though such things didn't interest us for long.

At twelve, we felt we belonged.
Not just to ourselves, but to each other.
The other a brother,
or more,
as we learned hobbies, games,
and the sorts of things
a mother can't teach her child.

His favorite was chess,
and he was the best.
He'd beat everyone who'd try to press
their bishops past the fourth rank. And, like
    a pony,
      he'd whinny and whinny,

as his knights would fork pieces.
He neglected Queens, preferring
Kings between royalty.

At sixteen, he got his first car. A beat up
    vanilla Mustang
bought with a jar of quarters and
the promise
to not go too far from home
with girls in the backseat.

He'd greet me with a smile.
I rode shotgun as we'd drive
    mile after mile,
down freeways and toll roads,
unknowingly.
I counted pennies so we could cross
the gate trolls which he'd file
as one of those jobs technology
should rapidly dispose of.

I was in love. And he knew it. He felt it too,
but after you show me yours
and I show you mine,
he said it was time to look past it,
and pick out which girls to bring to prom.

At twenty, I said goodbye to mom.
I was in school,
and such a fool to not
follow him into the army.

I studied math, and he went into
    the cavalry.
We'd
    write and write,
always in code.

"Don't ask,"
he begged. I promised,
    "I won't tell."
This is why being in love isn't soaring,
It's Hell.
It felt more like I fell
and couldn't get back up.

I remember the truck.
And the flag. I
    cried and cried.
The body bag was
never something I got to see.
Only a gold star in a window
greeted me. A
    rider-less cremello
pulled the hearse to a funeral
I wasn't allowed to attend.

At twenty-four,
I ended my life.
My strife found peace
when my hero released me
from pain without end. We
    laughed and laughed.

For years, I awaited the chance
to hold my Prince Charming again.
I met him not as an adversary, but
as a friend.
    "It has been too long,"
I said.
    "You always rode a pale horse."

Don't Talk To Me About Love

If you haven't fallen in love with an addict, don't talk to me about love.
Your Instagram romance is disposable and sad.
Selfies and memes make great Facebook posts
but I was there when my partner went mad.

If you haven't fallen in love with an addict, don't talk to me about love.
It's a word you can't begin to comprehend.
When the puking and shaking and trembling starts
you realize you're nowhere near the end.

If you haven't fallen in love with an addict, don't talk to me about love.
Your bad day is meaningless and bland.
Your boss may be an asshole, but I'm busy snatching
razor blades from my lover's hand.

If you haven't fallen in love with an addict, don't talk to me about love.
Your casino trip may mean you lose a grand,
but I was there when the money ran out
and found needles in my husband's nightstand.

If you haven't fallen in love with an addict, don't talk to me about love.
Your husband's friends may be a handful, it's true.
But I sometimes have to wonder if my man will make it home
in a single piece, or maybe, in two.

If you haven't fallen in love with an addict, don't talk to me
    about love.
Your man and you may occasionally fight,
but my husband and I still manage to make up
because most of all, I only care, that he's alright.

My Matador

Most people think of feet when dancing,
but I think of how your hands held mine.
I was so nervous, you so steady.
Each breath heavy as my fear got the best of me.
The methamphetamine clearly visible in your eyes.

I died that night. Me in dark, you in your suit of light.
You asked me to go to San Fermin to see the bull fights.
A red eye flight was easy for two men
selling chemistry to a world hooked on dope.

We drank red wine and coke.
You whispered in my ear how much you preferred
beef and beer, but we agreed the ham was simply divine.
I wanted a tattoo, and got in line behind a dozen or so
misspent youths not yet made rich with poor choices.

Their voices roared. Singing songs I couldn't understand
in unison. They demanded tears from even the most stern of
     hearts.
The matador's name, Padilla,
lost an eye in a previous fight
but graced the arena a final time.

His name and the eye patch were all I could understand.
We had no plans. Other than to run like Hell
when the crowd yelled, "Bull"
and to grab it by the horns in the brief time it passed us by.

I was drunk and in love. You bought some baggies of coke
to muddle by. You'd shoot it in the back of the hand
to hide the marks as bruises.
When asked about it, you'd say, "You shoulda seen the other guy."

I died that night. Each little death in a hotel bed
watching fireworks from a balcony
above the street where we ran for our lives.
Each stranger a friend, equally made men and women
who couldn't pretend to feel so alive.

The sky rained fire as we climbed over fences
and ran through alleyways of desire,
past the warning signs we couldn't read, nor cared to.

You kissed me as the heavens burned
in colors most never see. Each booming sound
a cacophony of pleasure unbounded.

I tried to bottle the emotions you gave me but
found few could handle the chemistry of something so strong.
Your face, a memory tied in my mind to
youthful exuberance and middle-aged treachery,
a formula so powerful it breaks my heart every time.

Each bull fight ended the same way.
The bull would sway as it was pierced by banderillas twice.
Once in my heart, and once in your hand.
We danced in Pamplona during San Fermin.
You had both my ears in hand as you finished me off
with a dance and not a fight.

You were the best matador.
I died that night.

There Is No God In Heaven

There is no God in Heaven.
He went down, chasing His best friend
who He last saw clinging to the stars—
on the greatest of falls.

Somewhere, He's lost in Perdition's maze,
screaming the name of his former lover
hearing nothing but the echo of an abyss.
A prison of infallible design.

Virgil was no help. Too tired to be a guide.
He lacked the trickster's eye
for which places were best to hide
from Judgement's omniscience.

They were both right.
To reign was well worth ambition.
But no army in Heaven, or Hell,
could fight the loneliness of eternity missing the other.

So God tried each station of torture.
Seeking to find the seed of the fruit,
which caused so much anger
and growth he could not help but love.

In his mind, Lucifer's found above
sitting in His throne,
crying alone,
missing Him,
wondering what war is worth being won.

Working Late In Silicon Valley

You have a habit of
working much later than I.

Today, you walked by me holding a coffee cup
and I fell in love with the dead
look in your eyes.
Dead. Not inanimate.

Eyes that once cupped a living soul,
dripped and empty, youthful bliss
seeping through the gaps
in your fingers. In need of the hard shake
of a triple espresso,
like a dog who played too long where
he shouldn't have been.

Perhaps, they spent
last night looking at
code. Diagrams of how the
universe is supposed to work.
Pouring over pages of instructions
whose source is your wellspring
of purpose and meaning.

Or maybe they were lost during
an entanglement with a lover.
Rivers and creeks overflowing
into the long hours of a night
that didn't begin until well

after your last code was checked in.
Experiencing fountains of youth that I hope
you can remember the taste of in your old age,
and occasionally get drunk in.

Meanwhile, I am ever so alert.
Not from stimulants, but from a good night's rest.
Storming down halls and climbing under desks,
fixing the world's much more inanimate problems.
Envious of your emptiness,
and dry of the recklessness
that staying up all night used to give me.

Perhaps, if I stare into your eyes long enough
I will understand what it is you see in the world,
decompiling the assembly and structure from your
perspective.

Or, I could learn her name,
whose curves you caressed
like the mug of that cup,
just a bit too long,
until you became the deceased man in front of me.
Drowning yet drained,
addicted to caffeine and embalming fluid
who can't wait to die again—
pouring yourself into yet another night.

Possession Of Love, On Trial

Punishment?
Is that what you think I need?
Is that what you think I deserve?
Can discipline correct such
wrongs with time
behind bars being served?

Can locking creatures like me
far, far away
from white picket fences,
into dark cells,
within darker prisons
right such terrible offenses?

Is that supposed to scare me? Or leave me bereft?
Putting me with thieves when I have nothing to steal,
rapists when I have no sex left,
murderers when I'm already so full of holes,
or mad men when I have no sense left.

Has it occurred to you that
of the countless people
who have sat in this chair,
in these robes,
facing the same doom,
for the same deed done,
before me who have replaced sexuality
with a chemical
that maybe one,

or more than one,
has lost their love instead?
I wear a letter so scarlet that it's infrared,
and see in colors you can only dread
in your greyscale nightmares.

My life is a horror show wearing
En Chroma glasses
and I am already in a prison
more vibrant than the masses
of beige tombs you can construct.
Mired in muck so dense you would think
a neutron star got sucked into a black hole
so deep no mental health professional can unfuck.

Did you ever wonder why it's called
falling in love?
The feeling of floating above when
your heart sinks that way it does
when some girl flirts with you?

And I hope that they do.

But when that happened to me
I was high.
The whole floor was ripped away,
and I soared into the sky like a rocket.
My eyes depressed into sockets from the
GI IB forces. My heart, pounding away
beating two-hundred beats per eternity
and a minute became longer than a day.

The sky warped, with my hope
of a normal romantic life
falling into decay well before
the crash
was coming along its way.

Sweat poured out as my heat shield
burned a fever so hot I melted into slag.
And you have the nerve to call me addicted?
Of course I am.

But perhaps you mistake the bang
of this judge's gavel
as a sonic boom
upon my return,
or a rocket, or a plane
reaching a particular speed.

In reality, the next sound you hear
is the very concept of speed itself.
Dissolved into the sound of my heart,
breaking,
into two grams' worth of tiny shards
you call evidence
because no one can find
another dark-haired boy with a smile,
kind enough to say hello to me
in a cozy bedroom
playing some One Republic MP3s
who asked if it was as good as I had expected.

You say I romanticize drugs.
But I say you know nothing
of either chemistry or love.
You believe both can be learned
in seventh grade
from teachers who recite
Romeo, or Juliet,
or Bohr, or Crick.

The bottle that once held lightning
cannot be relabeled for mere sand.
Because one hundred million volts
will turn it into glass so grand.
Petrified lightning is clear,
and like Narcissus and his pool
they fall endlessly into each other.
A molecule with colors you'll never understand.

Why else do tweakers love mirrors so?
And spend so much time in bed?
They call it glass, don't they?
We know it will kill us dead
because we already are.
It's not that we think your punishments are duller
but, tell me, sir,
describe to me the mirror's color
and I will show you a love
more beautiful than red.

Superman

I fucking hate Superman.
I always preferred Captain America.
Not that I can remember which one is DC or which one is
 Marvel.
I don't care about your franchise wars.
I just know that Captain America juiced.

Superman was born into perfection
an entire world away.
Empowered by a sun that no one can change the color of,
laughing every time someone threw a gun at him.
That isn't what I do when I see one pointed at me.

He'd bend steel pipes into prison bars for his foes
as if the world needed more of those in it.
His victims were just poor schmoes
robbing a bank for extra cash
like JP Morgan does every day
through the Federal Reserve Discount Window.

Captain America was a genetic concoction.
White out on top of a wimp who had nothing to live for.
Correction tape on the typewriter of history
a man becoming more than his original destiny.
He punched fucking Nazis.
And worked together as a team
instead of hogging the whole damned show.

Not that it matters which one I prefer.
I'm not the fastest,
or the strongest,
or the prettiest,
or the bravest,
or the anything-at-all-est.
Especially not anymore.

I just use my body to get my brain to meetings
and if I melt enough of it, maybe, I can just stay home instead.
That either makes me a villain,
or Professor X,
And I hope it's the former,
because I can't handle the thought of losing Magneto,
and the professor does way too much goddamned thinking
from a wheelchair.

Superman's only weakness is
that when he is near kryptonite
he is just like me—
    only handsom,
    with a long-term relationship,
    and friends at his work
    at the day job that he likes
    where his boss cares if he's sober that day.
    Looking at him through glasses he doesn't need
at unbloodshot eyes.

Maybe that's my problem in life.
I need more kryptonite.
Green. Black. White. Doesn't fucking matter at this point.

It does make me wonder if this is what it's like to feel like him.
The hero in the heroin.
Climbing roofs in a single bound.
Super hearing picking up strange voices from far away
after I've had more meth than I could fit onto a speeding train.

I can almost hear that woman in the distance,
crying for help from her derelict marriage
to a husband who's gone mad on some drug.
And I want to fly in and save her,
but today, I'm too fucking high.
Unable to find a telephone booth
where I can change into my normal self
without her hearing the quiver in my voice.

Too many fucking shards.
Too much kryptonite.
Meth was a drug made by some Nazi scientist
and I'm pretty sure Captain America is out to get me.
"I'll get you next time, Mr. Freeze!"
or was that fucking Batman?
I can't even keep up with my own goddamned poetry,
because today, I don't feel like Clark Kent.
Today, I feel like Christopher Reeves.

Who, now that I think about it, is just like Professor X
only with a melted brain.
Stripped of his honorific
and school for exceptional mutants.
After Magneto is long since gone.
Trapped to a wheelchair
hoping Captain America and the bank robbers
can remember who he used to be.

Square And Round Plates

Square plates go on the left.
Round plates go on the right.
Two separate sets from two separate grandparents.
Long since dead and buried. Now together.
Married. In my kitchen cabinet where they had been for years.

Next to the teacups.
China too fine for any visitor we would bring over.
Reserved for those nights where we'd watch
    The Crown,
    or *Downton Abbey,*
    or other shows featuring white British people
        doing the snobby things white British people must do.
Lifting our pinky fingers while we snuggled under a blanket.

Keeping us warm.
Like the dish water.
Rough hands and soft fingers taking turns
doing chores.
Washing on some days. Drying on others.
Mixing in champagne flutes or beer steins
depending how the last week went.
Feeling spent from a long domestic day
wrapped up by hanging the rag
on the oven handle with care.

Then that one thing happened.

Now,
a kitchen absent the sound
your wedding ring used to make on the sink.
Dry to the bone.
The dinnerware sets gathering dust
unused, unchipped, and yet broken.

And me.
At the dining room table.
Sitting on the only chair,
    with a package of discount ham and out-of-date sliced cheese
    (when I bother with the cheese),
        atop dollar store plastic bread packaging
        and store branded potato chips still left in the bag.
            Shattered into the tiniest of crumbs,
staring.
At the lonely expired muffin
preserved under a plastic Safeway container,
dried pieces of pastry keeping watch from on top.
Food for the roaches.
My only remaining company.

Vulnerability

I was used to being in control
of everything. Whether I wanted to be or not.
And now, I am not sure if I want it anymore.
I just want a boy to take charge,
whose actions I can trust will yield the specified results.

For him to take me by the arm in a way that I can trust his lead.
To fill me with meth, or salsa music.
Swaying with me to the beat in our shared mind
until I capitulate to his sense of control.
Exhausted at the thought of ever dancing again.

Until then, I will put these dark thoughts on a page,
scrawled on broken sheets of paper next to me
    while I sit in the shower, naked, with a stuffed unicorn,
    waiting for the cops to bust in and shoot at me
    for being too desperate for a prescription
    that they don't make anymore.

Writing the last words
I will never say.

One Night Stand

A novel is time committed,
beyond what most people plan.
If novellas are romance and weddings,
poems are my one night stand.

I remember the joy of chapters,
each one a promise made.
To grow and change a character
before the story should fade.

Poems need not players remembered,
identified on a stage.
Like radio blasts with no call sign,
no vows or rings exchanged.

With kinks and turns and twists,
named voltas and stanzas for rooms.
'Tis your fate that her fortune undresses,
not someone else's doom.

Author's soul and wit abandoned,
no quote marks or company
can prepare your ears for the lyrics
of her muttered ecstasy.

You think you know what you're doing.
But she's an older symphony.
You must speak her flute aloud—
no words read silently.

When she's done with you she'll dress
and depart without saying good bye.
You'll long for something substantial.

The Words I Don't Want To Say

Writers Of Substance

This list was compiled via good faith Internet and periodical research. No intention of libel or slander is meant against the families or descendants of these greats, and I have no problem publishing corrections should that ever be necessary in the future.

Additionally, it should not be concluded that this list is a recommendation by those on it to use substances or to break the law. I make no such suggestion myself. Many drugs, both legal and not, are in each category, and while some drank alcohol during Prohibition many were simply addicted to the bottle either before or after. It is also important to remember that some hard drugs like meth and cocaine were legally sold in the US during certain times. The botanical section, with the wide-spread yet incomplete legalization of marijuana is frankly impossible to comprehensibly compile.

All individuals have written at least one book (autobiographies count), even though writing may not be what they are popularly known for. Particularly the steroid users are, of course, better known for their physical characteristics than their writing. Steroids were also legal in the United States until around 1991.

Cocaine:
- Alister Crowley
- Elton John
- George Carlin
- Hunter S. Thompson
- Kate Moss
- Langston Hughes
- Sigmund Freud
- Steven King
- Steven Tyler
- Tim Allen

Speed (various forms):
- Ayn Rand
- Bob Dylan
- Hunter S. Thompson
- Jack Kerouac
- President John F. Kennedy
- Johnny Cash
- Luke Williams
- Nicholas Sheff
- Patrick Moore
- Phillip K. Dick
- Robert Downey, Jr.
- W. H. Auden
- Winston Churchill

Dissociatives (LSD/Mescaline/etc.):
- Aldous Huxley
- Aleister Crowley
- Allen Ginsberg
- Dr. Andrew Weil
- Hunter S. Thompson
- John Burnside
- John Lilly
- Ken Kesey
- Paul McCarthy
- Peter Matthiesen

Alcohol:
- Charles Bukowski
- Dylan Thomas
- Edger Allen Poe
- F. Scott Fitzgerald
- Jackson Pollock
- James Joyce
- John Burnside
- John Cheever
- Mark Rothko
- Mary Karr
- O. Henry
- T.S. Elliot
- Tennessee Williams
- Truman Capote
- William Faulkner

Botanicals (Pot/Hashish/etc.):
- Allen Ginsberg
- President Barack Obama
- Bill Maher
- Charles Baudelaire
- Dorothy Parker
- Earnest Hemingway
- Tommy Chong
- William Yeats

Steroids and Various Hormone Treatments:
- Gov. Arnold Schwarzenegger
- Chris Bell
- Dan Duchaine
- Floyd Landis
- Frank Zane
- Gregg Valentino
- Gov. Jesse Ventura
- Jose Canseco
- Louie Simmons
- Lyle Alzado
- Ronnie Coleman
- Sylvester Stallone

Opioids/Heroin/Painkillers/Prescription Drugs:
- Charles Dickens
- David Foster Wallace
- Elizabeth Barrett Browning
- Elvis Presley
- Herbert Selby

Jack Kerouac
Jim Morrison
John Cocteau
Marshall Mathers
Robert Downey Jr.
Samuel Taylor Coleridge
Thomas de Quincey
Thomas Kinkade

Also By Pill Press

Set during one of San Francisco's largest BDSM/leather events, Dore Alley, *American Dragon* is a tale of sex, drugs, and dance music. This dark romance is a revealing look at chemsex culture, the whirlwind world of gay hookups, and the ends that we're willing to go to in order to find someone just as insane as ourselves in the world.

Following is an excerpt from the novel.

ONE

It was fucking slow.

No one told me how thick the oil was. Despite my obsessive and meticulous research into thousands of bodybuilding forums, none of the countless posts had prepared me for this moment. My fiendish obsession had taught me the intricacies of diet, training, and even how to put together the perfect steroid cycle. Still, nothing in my collection of rapidly consumed knowledge mentioned getting fucking high-gauge needles so I could draw the shit out of the bottle.

It was over four years ago. God, I was such a rookie then. Everything I knew I read in a book or online. I think back to that version of me and realize how many obvious mistakes I made. There were so many "unknown unknowns" to deal with. But deciding to juice was a major step for me, and taking that first step was exhilarating as hell even though it frustrated me to no end to be missing this seemingly minor tool I could have so desperately used.

I paced angrily back and forth in my garage gym, nearly frothing at the mouth. After waiting for almost two months for the steroids to arrive from overseas, I was beyond eager to feel the testosterone flow through my veins. My eagerness manifested as stress against the syringe plunger, where tiny indentations had formed on my fingertips as they fought to fill the barrel with oil faster. I was enamored by the cottonseed oil, too dense for the meager twenty-five gauge needle which suspended pure masculinity in it.

Three bottles of testosterone cypionate, a handful of one milliliter syringes, and some Dianabol to kickstart the cycle were all part of the standard first-time user's kit. I had also opted to include the post-cycle therapy, and thus had Clomid on hand for when my cycle would be complete. I even added some testosterone freebase (TNE, they called it). I speculated my cycle would net me the guaranteed twenty pounds of muscle earlier than it could have if I left it off.

I was tired of being natural. Well, that's what I told myself at least. In reality, I was tired of waiting. Waiting to be happy with my body, or for some great power to will it into perfection. In high school, I was obese, but that was well behind me by then. To be honest, I got started in the gym to kill that guy. I hated him for being unpopular. Unloved. I was an egotist with nothing to be proud of, and a physique was as good a goal as any. After a few years of training and making some headway, I enjoyed being seen as someone who was fit though I still wasn't satisfied with myself. I had spent as many hours in the gym as my professional career could allow, but no matter how many hours I spent reading, lifting, and preparing my meals, I wasn't satisfied with the rate at which the results came. "Progress, not perfection," I heard the older lifters say, but I didn't care about them. No one did. It was the Age of Instagram after all. If I couldn't be as ripped as the gay porn actors I regularly jerked off to, what was the point of even showing up?

Fuck being fit. Freaks get the re-tweets.

And why shouldn't I start using steroids right away if that was my goal? I was twenty-four years old then, 170 pounds, and twelve percent body fat. Not world class, but I met all the broscience requirements to start juicing. I had no trophies or medals. At my best, I was good, not great. Maybe if I had better genetics or had been athletic when I was younger I wouldn't need the drugs. But who can pick their parents or go back in time?

Drugs were the perfect answer for people like me.

Instead of playing sports, my teen years were spent brooding in front of a computer, learning the ins and outs of a silicon era yet to be. How much time did I lose learning BASIC or C++, while the jocks played rugby or wrestled on the mats? How foolish could I have been, developing my mind while potential dating partners swiped left or right based upon facial features and muscular structures? I was angry at myself. I had wasted the one chance at adolescence I would ever have, and with it any chance to be one of the athletes I lusted after.

Fuck past decisions. Fuck being picked last for gym class. Fuck genetics. I, like God, refused to play with dice. Hormones weren't going to keep me from being what I wanted to be.

Muscular. Masculine. Powerful.

These were the attributes I saw on the Internet. The attributes society associates with successful men. And they were what I coveted as a homosexual. The only way for someone like me to get there was take control of biology away from Him through these drugs. I'd treat myself better than God did anyway.

There was no reason I couldn't become a model. Or a bodybuilder. Or any of the countless male body types that aroused me. I didn't need a coach or an overpriced personal trainer. I had done my homework and figured it all out.

It's true, you know, what they say about jocks—football players, wrestlers, doesn't matter—each is as stupid as a box of bricks, without exception. Most of them couldn't tell you anything about what's going on in the world, much less how they got such a marvelous physique. They were just winners in a genetic lottery. A lottery I had lost.

There were advantages to being an intelligent meathead. I just had to leverage them to outperform my competition.

They knew nothing of chemistry, biology, or physiology like I did. In this regard, I was better than them. Yet they were always more desirable than I'd ever be. At least bodybuilders took the time to learn what they were doing, and that difference was what attracted me to bodybuilding, both as a sport and a lifestyle. So I followed in their footsteps and became a willing acolyte. I devoured every bit of knowledge I could on nutrition, diet, and training regimens. From blog posts to medical journals, no source was left untouched.

Bodybuilding was a sport that felt like science. It was pure athleticism without the distraction of a game or a ball. My competition wasn't limited to a football field or wrestling mat. It was the whole damned world. The rules of engagement were as old as humanity itself, with the primary one being to outperform your competition. There were no yellow flags or foul lines. My priorities were clear. What I lost in time I would make up for with tenacity. Tenacity and drugs. I resolved to train smarter than my competition.

I would leverage economics and take advantage of the fact I could afford better drugs than the guy at home in his mother's basement. He spent his time playing sports instead of studying, so of course he should lose out. I was the better man. By extension, I should become the more confident one. The one in control.

I stared back at the syringe. So many thoughts and feelings were flooding my mind. Drop by agonizingly slow drop the oil filled the barrel. It took what seemed like an eternity before it approached full. It was my initiation, my first time. My self-doubts and ignorance returned with a rush. I found myself muttering.

"How exactly should one breathe before they stick themselves in the leg with a one-and-a-half-inch long needle? God, I hope I don't hit that nerve. Which one is it? The one that goes down the side of the leg, or the top? Fuck. Okay, sit down. Where's that video again? Thank God for transgender people posting their therapy videos online. Oh, hey, this doctor posted a better video still. Will I grow in my legs because that's where I do my shot?"

Fuck.

A streak of pain blasted through my body as the needle pierced the skin, though it quickly subsided. The further penetration into the meat of my quad was painless, but my hand quivered with every bit I pushed the needle deeper. I was convinced this was playing hell with my muscles.

"God . . . Is this happening? Maybe I shouldn't go in all the way to be safe. What the fuck does *aspirating* mean? Oh, like breathing, got it. No blood in the syringe is good. Well, that and who likes looking at blood anyway? Fuck it, here goes."

Despite the pain, I got hard. The idea of being filled with quintessential masculinity was overwhelming. I began to push the oil into my body. It was slow, though steady. I was such an eager student. An uneducated novice. After you do your first shot you're never natural again, and I was thrilled to cross that threshold. I envisioned the oil pumping my quads up in size. All I wanted in the world was to feel that oil inside me. I wanted to belong to the brotherhood of freaks and chemical bodybuilders.

And I got exactly what I wanted.

"Just a little bit more oil to go. I'm going to love this training session I can tell. I feel so huge already!"

I felt the plunger hit the end of the barrel. Even the discomfort of removing the needle too quickly didn't stop me from shooting my load.

All over the rubberized floor.

My leg muscles tensed slightly when I came. In the needle's place was a small droplet of blood dripping down my leg.

I capped the needle quickly, threw the syringe to the side, then walked a few steps. I sensed the distinct taste and smell of pine needles. It was the newfound flavor of masculinity. I marveled at these new sensations and the slippery puddle of jizz on the floor.

"That was . . . unexpected," I said, licking my lips.

While I knew some drugs could leave a weird taste in your mouth, I didn't think steroids would be one of them. From the research I've done in the years since this first experience with a needle, few ever describe it the same way. Anecdotally, tastes and smells are as unique as the individual bodybuilders themselves.

Hobbling to the kitchen, I grabbed a paper towel to wipe the blood off my leg and my sperm off the floor.

Feeling ever so alive, I took the time for obligatory self-worship in the mirror. Naked and still bleeding down my leg, I rotated through all of the classic bodybuilding poses. Rear triceps. The lat spread. The side chest. Each gave me a chance to validate my newly discovered superiority and manhood. I took the time to examine each body part and allowed my imagination and excitement to swell with possibilities. Finally, I savored my relative size in the front double bicep pose, as my arms were my best feature. Short, military-style, buzz cut hair gave me an edgy look that allowed me to pass as somewhat older.

I resigned to pick up some weight. I curled a few warm-up sets with the mismatched pair of dumbbells I had, imagining the work my tendons and muscle fibers must be doing under the skin to make such motion a reality. Feeling confident with a slight pump, I put the dumbbells down and went to the bench press in the corner of my gym. Its cushion was worn from the previous owner and offered little support to whoever used it. The plates sure felt lighter, though to this day I am unsure how much of that was the drugs or my excitement. Either way, I added an extra plate to the bench press and went on to torture myself for being too small—a torture marked with heavy grunting and half-reps which further fueled my testosterone-aided ambitions.

For the rest of the night, the clatter of plates echoed in my gym as bars were loaded and cable machine handles were swapped out with increased frequency. Feeling perfectly in control of my body and destiny, and armed with some no-name knockoff foreign steroid bottles, I knew that the perfect body was just a matter of time away.

Well, time and drugs, anyway.

www.ingramcontent.com/pod-product-compliance
Lightning Source LLC
Chambersburg PA
CBHW071405080526
44587CB00017B/3180